The St. Monica Ministry

Spiritual Exercises to Help with a Loved One's Faith Crisis

By Jack Buchner

Cathedral Foundation Press

Printed and bound in the United States of America

2 3 4 5

ISBN 1-885938-13-6

Library of Congress Catalog Card Number: 98-071690

Published in 1998 and 2010 by

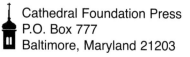 Cathedral Foundation Press
P.O. Box 777
Baltimore, Maryland 21203

Publisher: Christopher Gunty
Cover Design: Lisa Wiseman
Printed By: Catholic Printing Services

Table of Contents

When I feel guilty for something I did or did not do for my loved one --- is it _Rational_ or _irrational_?

Place my perceived failures at the cross so Jesus can transform me and give me a greater giftedness so I can share that with the world.

FOREWORD

Happiness is open to us only if we keep open the doors of our heart, if we are ready to hear and if we do not bolt ourselves in. It is very easy to turn in on ourselves and focus on our pain when a loved one is indifferent to God and the Church.

This text is intended to assist the reader to realize that God uses every event and circumstance of life to deepen the intimacy of the relationship that God wishes to bring about with each of us. Therefore, we should be people of hope, not despair. Leo Buscaglia has written:

> "As long as we have hope, we have direction, the energy to move, and the map to move by. We have a hundred alternatives, a thousand paths and an infinity of dreams. Hopeful, we are halfway to where we want to go, but hopeless, we are lost forever."

Yet, as G.K. Chesterton in his usual paradoxical style has said: "Hope only becomes a virtue, when the situation is hopeless!"

The theological virtue of hope is an inner power which flows from faith in the promises of Christ. This living faith is the confident assurance that what we hope for will come to pass (Heb 11:1). Such hope is a gift. One does not acquire that kind of certainty and confidence except by God's grace. This points to the importance of prayer. As we read in Matthew's Gospel: Ask and it shall be given to you (Mt 7:7).

Each of us has been given a particular mission in our life to fulfill. It involves the happiness of ourselves and others now and in the future. God wishes to work through us, providing the strength, courage and vision we need. People who are filled with divine hope tend to think, pray and work more effectively as co-workers with the Lord in bringing about a better, happier world.

Pope John Paul II, addressing a Youth Rally during his visit to Los Angeles in 1987:

> "If we look only at ourselves with our limitations and sins, we quickly give way to sadness and discouragement. But if we keep our eyes fixed on the Lord, then our hearts are filled with hope. We cannot live without hope. We have to have some purpose in life, some meaning to our existence. Without hope we begin to die."

This book is intended to assist the reader in reviewing critical elements of worship, faith and prayer that renew this virtue of hope in those distressed or worried about a loved one's response to the ultimate questions of life.

A second benefit of this manuscript is the reminder that our sojourn through life is that of journey. I'm told that there is a sign on a bridge in Denmark which says, "Life is a bridge. Do not build your house on it."

So where are we? In constant need of God's help; all of us. We all need the love of friends and faith in a loving God to sustain us. We need a believing and loving community to count us as one of them, and to bear us up.

Traveling through life isn't primarily about changing places. It's deepening the values and ideals of Christ ever further into my being. We do this well when we do it with one another with deep faith in God and prayer focused on God. When this happens our response to loved ones will be God's intended response. For the proper response to the ever-deepening experience of divine love is to transform it into human love for one another. The energy and inspiration of this human love will be perceived as divine. Your light must shine in the sight of others, so that, seeing your good works, they may give the praise to your Father in heaven (Mt 5:16).

In writing this book, I want to acknowledge two special sources. First, I would like to thank Dr. David Jeremiah and his work titled "Prayer: The Great Adventure" for contributing to the ideas on forgiveness as found in Matthew's Gospel and presented in the introduction to this text.

Second, the background information on St. Monica, as expressed in this text's introduction, is found in "Healing The Original Wound" by Benedict J. Groeschel, CFR (Servant Publications, Ann Arbor, Michigan, 1993).

Jack Buchner
May 1998

INTRODUCTION

*T*he Monica ministry is a pastoral outreach to all those adults who have friends and relatives who are not active in their practice of the faith at this time. For many of these adults this experience is a source of hurt and deep disappointment. Many times these people wonder: "How can this be?" or "Why is this happening?" or "What can I do about this?"

While there are many responses to these and associated questions, the Monica ministry, developed around the life experiences of St. Monica, suggests that the best response is to use this experience as a means of drawing closer to Christ **yourself.** This not only is what our call to sainthood is all about, but also, in becoming more Christ-like ourselves, we permit our Lord to be reflected more clearly through us to others, including our inactive relatives and friends, and thus touch them in the way and time of His choosing.

Following an overview on the life of St. Monica, our suggested response will include four additional sections. These other chapters include:

1) why hurting is legitimate when loved ones do not attend Mass

2) faith – its purpose and role in our lives

3) prayer – its essence and necessity

4) pastoral responses to commonly asked questions

The Monica ministry will highlight the virtues of faith and prayer, and assist participants to become more like St. Monica in their conviction that the grace of Christ will change hearts and lives.

Chapter One

The Making of a Saint

*I*n Rome, there is a small chapel with a tomb which serves as the burial place of a woman who died 1,600 years ago. That woman is St. Monica. I'm told that lovely frescoes decorate the walls of the chapel. One shows her weeping and being consoled by a bishop. When he asked Monica why she was crying, the distraught woman answered, "I'm crying for my son." The bishop said, "Don't worry. The son of these tears will not be lost."[1]

Her son had his own ideas. As a matter of fact, his rebellion worsened year after year. Rather than cooperating with the grace of God, he angrily rebuked the mother who reached out to him in the love of God. Did this stop Monica? Not for an instant.

Not only was her son a serious concern, Monica was married to an abusive husband as well. Instead of drowning in her own sorrow, this saintly woman never stopped praying for both of her loved ones. Shortly after his baptism, Monica's husband became ill and was prepared to die. God also answered Monica's prayers for her son, and we know him as St. Augustine. God heard this wonderful woman's tearful prayers – the prayers of a lifetime, the prayers of a persistent widow and mother.

Jesus told his disciples a parable about persisting in prayer and not losing heart:

In a certain city there was a judge who neither feared God nor regarded man; and there was a widow in that city who kept coming to him and saying, "Vindicate me against my adversary." For a while he refused; but afterward he said to himself, "Though I neither fear God nor regard man, yet because this widow bothers me, I will vindicate her, or she will wear me out by her continual coming."

And the Lord said, "Hear what the unrighteous judge says. And will not God vindicate his elect, who cry to him day and night? Will he delay long over them? I tell you, he will vindicate them speedily. Nevertheless, when the Son of Man comes, will he find faith on earth?" (Lk 18:2-8)

God wants us to be persistent. There is a big difference between the actual and permissive will of God. The actual will of God decrees events. The permissive will of God allows events. We need to remember that whatever happens, God is with us.

I'm sure there were many times when St. Monica was tempted to wonder if anyone cared. Her husband was a pagan for years. Her son, by his own admission, was worse than a pagan. These loved ones probably considered her a religious fanatic and busybody. Hardly anyone else paid much attention, except for two bishops who were moved to compassion by her prayers.

Meanwhile, Monica became one of the first people to receive Holy Communion daily. In her day, Mass was not said in all churches every day, only on Sundays, Holy Days, and at funerals. Monica apparently would get hold of the obituary from the town crier and make it to a funeral every day. She would make a circuit of different churches to make sure she attended the liturgy.[2]

Monica is a saint of faith and prayer and tears. Her symbol is a handkerchief. If you see a statue of a woman holding a handkerchief, that's Monica. This devout mother didn't think her son gave a hoot, and most of the time he probably didn't. But out of the corner of his eye, the rebellious and stubborn young man must have watched his mother.

Only a few months before her death, Augustine told his mother of his conversion. "She was filled with triumphant exultation, and praised you, O Lord, who are mighty beyond what we ask or conceive: for she saw that you had given her more than with all her pitiful weeping she had ever asked. You had converted me to yourself." [3]

Augustine himself would become one of the greatest composers of prayers in church history. Who taught him to pray? A woman who ten thousand times must have said, "My God, my God, why have you forsaken me?"[b]

Don't ever give up on people you know! No matter how far from God, they seem to be. No one can hide beyond the reach of God. Psalm 139 offers these comforting words:

> "Yahweh, you examine me and know me,
> You know if I am standing or sitting,
> You read my thoughts from far away,
> whether I walk or lie down, You are watching,
> You know every detail of my conduct.
> The word is not even on my tongue,
> Yahweh, before You know all about it;
> close behind and close in front You fence me around,

shielding me with Your Hand.
Such knowledge is beyond my understanding,
a height to which my mind cannot attain.
Where could I go to escape Your spirit?
Where could I flee from Your presence?"

Jerusalem Bible

If there is someone you know and love who has strayed from God, keep praying. Don't ever lose hope. Unite yourself ever-more deeply with Jesus, especially in the Eucharist.

The Eucharist is a most special blessing to us. The Eucharist permits us to prayerfully enter into an intimate association with Christ. Somehow, when we are hurting, we are capable of engaging in deeper levels of meditation and thanksgiving. Our present circumstances (as we think about our adult children who are not sharing in the Eucharist) influence our experience of what it means to be one with the suffering Christ.

Participation in the Eucharist is a mystical, yet concrete, way of internalizing the suffering love of our Lord. Through silent meditation and reflective prayer, we experience a spiritual touching of Christ's wounds. Also, the broken bread and the spiritual drink enable us to probe our own brokenness and find strength in the power of the risen Christ. The Eucharist also brings forgiveness through oneness with Jesus Christ.

Another dimension of the Eucharist is unity, which is vividly communicated when individuals from different backgrounds come together to celebrate as members of one body. This mystical communion reveals that there is one Spirit and one Church. In fact, only the Holy Spirit can bring together the multitude of differences that are found in humanity. This diversity, united through the one Spirit, manifests the creativity, beauty, and power of almighty God; and unity provides a strong witness of His transforming presence in the world.

The extremes found in individuals and families make the Eucharist a crucial focus of the **Monica** ministry. In the unity of Holy Communion, there is a love and equality that tears down the many barriers that separate people. Through this sacrament, we realize the power of diversity. Because the Eucharist exemplifies the diversity found in Jesus Christ, we come to understand that the church is a mystical communion[7] that can only be made through the Spirit of Christ. This truth should lead us to examine our inner lives, which is yet another dimension of the cross.

Intentionally missing Mass on Sunday or other holy days of obligation can never be condoned or rationalized, but the Church should direct offenders toward a spirituality that reunites them in the Body of Christ. Through God's loving action, all past sins can be turned into God's greater glory by equipping people to reach out to others who experience the same failings. As St. Paul informs us in Romans 8:28: "We know that by turning *everything* (emphasis mine) to their good God co-operates with all those who love him, with all those that He has called according to his purpose."

Every situation allows for personal transformation, growth and outreach to others. Whenever we think about giving up on others, we need to remember that God never gave up on us. Just as Christ reaches out in forgiveness and identifies with humanity through his own wounds, those who follow Him must do the same. The Eucharist draws us to Christ and sends us to others, including others who need to be forgiven and perhaps encouraged to participate in the sacrament of Reconciliation before returning to Mass and Communion.

In Matthew 6:12, we read about forgiveness in the context of the Lord's Prayer. Then in verse 14, Jesus returns to this particular (forgiveness) part of the prayer stating: "Yes, if you forgive others their failings, your heavenly Father will forgive you yours, but if you do not forgive others, your Father will not forgive your failings either." Of all the verses in the prayer, of all of the sections in the prayer, this is the only one Jesus returns to for emphasis. It's as if He's saying to us, **please don't miss this**. This is critical.

As someone once said, that if you can get your arms around this, you can learn to get along with anybody all the time. What a great thought!

This part of the Lord's prayer puts into our minds a consciousness of sin. For we're not talking about overspending here when we read "debts." This means trespass, and the Lucan translation says "sins." He's talking about those who sin against us. He's talking about the evil in the world, those who do evil things. And if nothing else, when we pray this prayer each day, we remember that we live in a graced yet fallen world. But this is not about the consciousness of sin. This is about the confession of it. In Matthew 6:14-15, Jesus gives a commentary that, when we seek forgiveness for our own sin, we are to forgive those who have sinned against us. Our relationship with the Lord can't be right until our relationship with others is made right.

Furthermore, in Matthew 5:23-24, Jesus says if you bring your gift to the altar and remember someone has something against you, leave your gift, "go and be reconciled with your brother first, and then come back and present your offering."

The Talmud, the rabbinical commentary on the Old Testament, says, He whose will is indulgent toward other's faults will be mercifully dealt with by the supreme judge Himself.

Jesus says, if you want to be known as a child of God, walk around with a spirit of forgiveness in your heart because that gives you away.

beautiful

In Ephesians 4:32, Paul says we are to forgive, even as God, for Christ's sake, has forgiven us. That's the standard!

Proverbs 19:11 says it is the glory of a man to pass over a transgressor. There is something very special about a person who learns about forgiveness.

But if Jesus included it in his prayer and commented about it after his prayer, He illustrated it masterfully with the story He told in Matthew 18:15-23, the story of seventy times seven. He illustrated it again in the story of the servant who owed the King 10,000 talents. That would be so much money it would be hard for us even to conceive. How could a servant ever get into that kind of trouble? But he did. He had **nothing** with which to pay. But, he says to the King, have patience with me, and I'll pay you all. (We almost want to laugh out loud.) He would have to live 190 years and put every dime he ever earned into his debt. This man was a fool, no matter how you look at it.

So the King knows he can't pay; the debt is too great, and so he says I'm going to forgive you all. Now, the King represents God. The servant represents all of us. We owed a debt we could not pay, and He forgave. How could he forgive a debt as astronomical as that? How could He cope with a debt that was so great? He sent his own Son who went to the cross and let Him die.

And the story goes that the forgiven servant went out, and

some who owed him a paltry sum compared to that for which he had been forgiven, came to him and asked for forgiveness. He demanded that they pay all. And the King was furious. And he had him brought back in and put him in prison. And the moral is: so my heavenly Father will do the same to you, unless you forgive from your heart.

We are to forgive others, because we ourselves are forgiven so very much. And if we will not forgive them, we will never **experience** the joy of the forgiveness which is ours from God through Christ.

And we've been forgiven so much, how could there be anything too great that would slip out from the category of God's forgiveness?

What else does this passage teach us?

1. We are to forgive **because** we are forgiven much.
2. We are to forgive just as we are forgiven. Fully. Unconditionally.
3. We are to forgive that we might be forgiven.
4. We are to forgive **before** we need to be forgiven.

What **is** going on here? How can our forgiveness of others in any way condition God's forgiveness of us? If we don't seek interpersonal forgiveness, it will get in the way of our openness to experiencing God's forgiveness of ourselves. God wants us to take the forgiveness we've received, and pass it out to those who need it in our lives. This includes our adult children who no longer practice their religion.

American pastoral theologian Louis Snead says that Jesus takes the hardest trick in the bag, forgiveness, and insists that we perform it. Or we're out in the cold. **Jesus** knows that it is a matter of incongruity to receive his forgiveness and not pass it along to others. So the only way we can heal the hurt of the pain that will not heal itself is to forgive the person who hurt us. Forgiving stops the re-runs. Forgiving changes our memory's vision. When we release the wrongdoer from the wrong, we cut a malignant tumor out of our life.

Therefore, as followers of Jesus, it is important for us to forgive loved ones for their seeming indifference to the practice of the faith. It is also important for these loved ones to **experience** that forgiveness from us so that in turn, this experience may facilitate their coming to forgive whomever or whatever it is that is preventing them from joining wholeheartedly into the life of the parish. Practically speaking, there are four stages of forgiveness:

1. When we're trying to figure out how to deal with forgiveness, the first stage we go through is the stage of hurt. Forgiveness starts with the feeling of the pain.

2. After hurt comes some form of hatred. We can't shake the memory of how much we were hurt. We want the person to suffer as we are suffering.

3. Healing. Taking on the new lenses that will enable us to see the person who hurt us in a whole new light. And we turn back the flow of pain, and we're free. By the grace of God, I forgive.

4. The coming together again. Sometimes the person comes back into our lives. Sometimes not. But that's the process.

The Church, in fact, urges us to pray the Lord's Prayer sincerely **each** day because it is likely that sometime today someone will do something mean or nasty to me and I need to ask God to give me a forgiving spirit. And then when somebody does something to us we can say to them, I've already forgiven you. Can you imagine God permitting you to create that kind of spirit within you each day?

Jesus said that those who live by God's forgiveness must imitate it, and that our only hope is to come to grips with this truth: we can not hold faults against others when our faults haven't been held against us.

An old, anonymous poem I found reads this way:

>Forgive our sins as we forgive.
>You taught us Lord to pray,
>but you alone can grant us grace to live the
>   words we say.
>How can your pardon reach and bless
>   the unforgiving heart?
>That broods on wrongs and will not let
>   old bitterness depart.
>In blazing light, your cross reveals
>   truth we dimly know.
>How much the debts people owe to us.
>   How great our debt to you.

That's it: The real secret to forgiving others is the Holy Cross. Whenever you feel it's too tough to forgive, go to the cross. In the light and power and spirit of the cross, we can turn to others and say you are forgiven. I forgive you.[a]

In our Catholic tradition, this experience of forgiveness often includes the wonderful gift of the sacrament of Reconciliation. Let us briefly revisit the meaning this sacrament has in our lives by first reflecting upon our own understanding of the significance of forgiveness and reconciliation in our everyday lives. Let us revisit the role of the priest in sacramental reconciliation and the role of the penitent so that with confidence, conviction and sensitivity to the timing of the Holy Spirit, we may perhaps lead our loved ones to experience of Christ in this sacrament and then to the Eucharist.

It is understood that the ordained priest is authorized to offer sacramental absolution. Too often, though, we misunderstand this ministry as a restriction of the power and obligation of people to forgive one another. But if we understand what absolution means, we can see that this special role of the priest does not at all interfere with our loving forgiveness of each other.

When the priest offers absolution, he acts with an official mandate from the Christian community to welcome a person to the Eucharistic table. To give absolution is to accept a person as a full member of the people of God. From this, it is clear that only a commissioned minister can speak in the name of the complete community. Absolution thus stresses the communal dimension of the love of God. Absolution completes the celebration of the sacrament by making it known that the forgiving love of God is present and should be present in the whole community.

ask Jack

When I sin against anyone, I sin against everyone. If I harm someone, then due to the guilt I experience, my feelings, my self-occupation that results after the action, I find that I am not as "available," not as open to all others as I otherwise would be. It is impossible for me to go around to every individual who touches my life after I've sinned and say that I'm sorry, I'm not fully available to you right now. Therefore, it is good for me to have the sacramental encounter with someone who:

– accepts me as I am
– is authorized by the community to speak and act on its behalf

    – can assist me in looking at my action and facilitating a constructive change

    – welcomes me back to the community once more as a full and loved member

Preparing for an honest participation in the sacrament begins with an acknowledgement of our shortcomings and of being sorry for them. It is a grace for any of us to acknowledge that we need Jesus Christ in our lives. It is also a grace for anyone of us to know that we can share our thoughts about our sinfulness with some person through whom God's love will show. This is why you and I need to have a sense of freedom in our "confessing" to another person, the priest.

Furthermore, my sharing ought to be motivated by a sincere desire on my part to reform my life, that is, to live differently than I am presently. This may mean, for example, that I need to look at myself differently: that is, as someone who is deeply loved by God and not as a worthless failure. It may mean that I need to look at other people more sincerely as brothers and sisters in Christ and not primarily as competitors or objects to be used. It may mean that I need to look more closely at the relationships that I now have in my life in terms of their quality and not so much at the quantity of things I possess.

Additionally, as I more and more allow God to transform me, I need to let the healing take place. I need to allow God to heal me at times when God and others forgive me, but I somehow won't forgive myself. I have a need for self-forgiveness. I also need to create the conditions where others, through me, can truly feel God's healing. When this happens, people begin to see the next stage in their life with a new outlook from which everyone, indeed the world, benefits.

18

The rites of the sacrament, presently approved for use in the United States, are these three:

a) Reconciliation for individual penitents

b) Reconciliation with a small group of penitents which includes individual confession

c) Reconciliation for a large group with general confession and absolution

Let's look briefly at all three rites.

A. Reconciliation With Individual Penitents

Reconciliation with individual penitents was modified primarily to emphasize that sacraments are rituals to be celebrated. This sacrament is no exception. Walking into a room where there is a comfortable atmosphere, the option of sitting in a chair for face-to-face dialogue with a confessor or staying behind a screen makes the experience of participating in this sacrament more liberating, a real affirmation of human dignity.

B. Reconciliation With Small Groups of Penitents

Reconciliation with a small group of penitents, which includes individual confession, is the second approved rite. The rite combines both the communal act and the personal act which are both so integral to the nature of sin and reconciliation. The rite begins with the song followed by the presider welcoming everyone to the celebration and explaining the purpose of the rite. After a short prayer, attention focuses on the Word of God and a homily. A communal examination of conscience adapted to the age and background of those assembled is then undertaken. Next the penitents go to the confessors for individual confession.

C. Reconciliation With a Large Group of Penitents

This option is very limited at the present time. While many pastors would like to offer this form of the sacrament regularly, present regulations require that Reconciliation for a large group with a general confession and absolution be used only when it is impossible (physically or otherwise) to accommodate individual confessions. At times, it may be lawful and even necessary for a priest or bishop to give general absolution to a group of people. In such a rite, penitents should prepare well through an examination of conscience and fulfill the conditions of sorrow for sin and resolve to avoid committing them again. Also, serious sins should be confessed by individuals as soon as the circumstances permit.

The variety in the rites for the sacrament of Reonciliation is a sign that God's loving forgiveness can come to us in many ways.

Chapter Two

Your Hurt is Legitimate
What the Mass Means to Catholics

"In the Church's liturgy the divine blessing is fully revealed and communicated. The Father is acknowledged and adored as the source and the end of all the blessings of creation and salvation. In his Word who became incarnate, died, and rose for us, he fills us with his blessings. Through his Word, he pours into our hearts the Gift that contains all gifts, the Holy Spirit."

Paragraph 1082
Catechism of the Catholic Church

The Bible presents God as the ultimate end to which all else is relative and pen-ultimate. The Scripture urges us to give absolute loyalty to the absolute and relative loyalty to the relative. So when we make the relative absolute we are in deep trouble. Among other benefits, authentic worship at Mass is meant to safeguard against such distortions. The Mass points us to the person of Jesus. It brings His words and His presence among us.

The lesson for Catholics is that worship at Mass has two sides. It is not strictly a means to an end. Prayerful participation at Mass is a proper end in itself. At Mass, we celebrate the greatness of God, the love of Christ, the power and presence of the Holy Spirit, and the worth of each other.

Logic demands, however, that if we worship Him who is Creator and Lord of both heaven and earth, we must concern ourselves with His creation. Our spiritual intimacies must affect our domestic manners. Worship is our generative experience. If we worship a God who is just, we must be committed to work for justice. If we worship a God who is love, we must be loving in our relationships. If we worship a God who cares for all whom He has made, we cannot be indifferent to our brothers and sisters in their need. When we lift up our minds, hearts and souls to God at Mass, we affirm our active participation in life, not justify our withdrawal from it.

How can we speak of and respond meaningfully to a God who is real in our lives, and who is the Providence out of which our life springs? Until we start thinking seriously about these questions, our participation at Mass will only be externally proper, but the God to which it is meant to point will be absent. The ability to ask this question is essential to a sincere effort to think through the nature of reality. We hope our liturgy is ordered to reflect reality, for the Church helps us to understand God and His world in such a way that we reflect our faith in **everything** we say and do. In other words, until we grasp the central meaning of our celebration, we shouldn't concern ourselves with the external structures and language of the Mass.

Let me bring this to a conclusion by emphasizing two primary and fundamental points about worship at Mass.

First, our participation at Mass is something we do for God. We are prone to be far too self-oriented in our worship, even though our demeanor has a communal look. Sometimes we ask, "What will the Mass do for me?" The Mass, however, is our response to what God has done and is doing for us in Christ Jesus. In a realistic sense, it does have something to do with broken faith and loyalty, failing grades, a faltering career, the balance in my checkbook, or problems with the in-laws. But because our prayers and praise are something we do for God, worship at Mass transcends our fleeting moods out of love. Nothing we set ourselves to do every week at a certain hour would be equally enjoyable every time. We do not always feel like being in church. Participating actively at Mass, however, is something we do for God. And I can agree with the saying that you don't have to go to church to be a Christian. But you do have to participate actively in the sacrifice of the Mass to be a Catholic, unless you're seriously ill. It is integral to our identity. Yes, it is cute to say "You can be in communion with God while walking in the woods breathing in the beautiful nature of God." Perhaps this is true. However, we never want to confuse worship of creation with the proper worship of the Creator. Moreover, at Mass we pray together in the midst of Christ's presence, which is sacramental.

> "...because his mystery of salvation is made present there by the power of his Holy Spirit; because his Body, which is the Church, is like a sacrament (sign and instrument) in which the Holy Spirit dispenses the mystery of salvation; and because through her liturgical actions the pilgrim Church already participates, as by a foretaste, in the heavenly liturgy."

Paragraph 1111
Catechism of the Catholic Church

Secondly, the Mass is something we do together and for each other. All of us are involved. Mass is not a performance

[handwritten margin note: At last! The answer to my son the Naturalist!]

by a few for the many. <u>It's what we are together that counts.</u> <u>We may seek God alone, but we worship Him in common.</u>

Even before Mass begins, as we gather at the church, we greet one another. This is so very important. We take time to listen to the hearts of our brothers and sisters. This greeting and listening is an occasion when, figuratively, <u>we put our ear</u> <u>close to our neighbor's heart so that we can hear the pains and</u> <u>the hopes, the anguish and the possibilities in their lives</u>, the states of being we are all bringing to the setting. Even though the consecration really occurs even when we don't reach out as we should, our appreciation of what really takes place at each Mass is lessened somewhat without our whole-hearted response to the reality we celebrate. <u>The love of God, neigh-</u> <u>bor and self that is awakened in genuine prayer at Mass is a</u> <u>continuous process.</u> Each aspect of love is connected with the other. The ultimate task of making the Mass meaningful and relevant will not solely be in the development of new forms but in the creation of a new people: new people **in** the Body of Christ, serving God and one another as the Body of Christ. Truth in the abstract is a wonderful thing. Truth acted upon, most perfectly at Mass, is a most satisfying experience.

You acknowledge and probably agree with much of what has been written. But, specifically, how can your understand- ing of the Mass assist your own spiritual growth <u>as you think</u> <u>about your adult child who is not sharing in the Eucharist?</u> Participation in the Eucharist is a mystical, yet concrete, way of internalizing the suffering love of our Lord. Through silent meditation, reflective and communal prayer, we experience a spiritual touching of Christ's wounds. Also, the Eucharist and the Precious Blood enable us to probe our own broken- ness and find strength in the power of the risen Christ. The

Eucharist brings forgiveness through oneness with Jesus Christ.

Another dimension of the Eucharist is unity, which is vividly communicated when individuals from different backgrounds come together to celebrate as members of one body. This mystical communion reveals that there is one Spirit and one church. In fact, only the Holy Spirit can bring together the multitude of differences that are found in humanity. This diversity, united through the one Spirit, manifests the creativity, beauty and power of Almighty God; and unity provides a strong witness of his transforming presence in the world.

The different personalities and types of people coming to your church make the Eucharist a crucial focus of all the parish's ministry. In the sacred oneness of Holy Communion there is a love and equality that tears down the many barriers that separate people. Through this sacrament we realize the power of diversity. Because the Eucharist exemplifies the diversity found in Jesus Christ, we come to understand that the Church is a mystical communion that can **only** be made through the power of the Holy Spirit. This truth should lead us to examine our inner lives, which are yet another dimension of the cross. Do we truly believe that the blood of Christ was shed for all sins, and his healing excludes no one? Every word, each action, all situations in our lives allow for personal transformation, growth and outreach to others. Whenever we think about giving up on another human being, we need to remember that God never gave up on us. Just as Christ reaches out in forgiveness and identifies with humanity through his own wounds, those who follow him must do the same. The Eucharist draws us to God and sends us to others.

The crux of the matter

Our worth, or that of any other person, must never be categorized or prioritized according to socioeconomic standing, or (moral) behavior. Rather, the church calls us to see others as deeply loved by God and to respond to their needs in the best way possible.

Interestingly, *Lamentations* was written in the context of community. American pastoral theologian Eugene Peterson provides us with some noteworthy points:

> When biblical people wept, they wept with their friends... The biblical way to deal with suffering is to transform what is individual into something corporate... Response to suffering is a function of the congregation. Most cultures show a spontaneous comprehension of this. The suffering person is joined by friends who come together in a communal lament. They do not hush up the sound of weeping but augment it. They do not hide the sufferer away from view of anyone... when others join the sufferer, there is consensual validation that the suffering means something... When suffering cannot be expressed emotionally, there is a consequent inability to recover... Further, community participation insures a human environment.[5]

Most biblical images of religious identity are related to community life; for example, the Bible presents images of Israel as a family, a kingdom, a covenant, a banquet, one vine with many branches, a body with many parts, a chosen race, and a royal priesthood.[6] Peterson states that the biblical view of humanity is "person-in-community – a people of God." He writes that:

> The essential reality of humanity is corporate...Adam

was not complete until there was Eve. The meaning is clear: no individual is complete in himself, in herself; humanity is person-in-relationship. Persons are always part of community even when they deny it, even when they don't know it.[7]

Catholic unity has its human beginnings in the triune God who separated and emptied himself to bring new life to humanity. Like a loving parent who suffers radical surgery to give a vital organ to a dying child, so it is with God who gave himself that humanity might live in wholeness, in a common-union, a communion.

The Eucharist calls us to be a fellowship of compassion and tolerance, a community where members can experience acceptance and self-worth. But this is only possible if people increase in love for God and their neighbors. Sin wears many faces, but its root is a lacking in the experience of God's love within us.

In summary, then, the Mass is our source of life, for life. We are called to worship in community, centered in Christ, by our very nature. Something is amiss when a Catholic freely misses Mass. When this person is a son or daughter, we have a right to feel badly about this situation. However, this very situation provides a unique opportunity for our own spiritual growth. It can enable us to touch the sufferings of Christ, and experience his healing presence. It can deepen our prayer. It offers us themes for personal meditation. It allows us to see ourselves as totally dependent upon God, and yet willing participants in the action of His grace.

REFLECTION QUESTIONS

1. How truly present am I at Mass? Do I listen attentively to the Scriptures? Where are my thoughts during the consecration? Do I see the offertory gifts are representative of my life, and as being joined with Christ in an offering to God? What meaning does this have for me? What role does my prayer of thanksgiving after communion play in my life? How do I cooperate with the effects of the grace of the Mass after I leave church? How does it relate to my adult children who do not practice the faith?

2. Have I ever given up on my adult children? On myself? What might this suggest about the depth of my faith? What is God asking me to do about this?

3. Am I more and more willing to "let go and let God" in my life? Do I trust that all that happens is in God's hands?

Chapter Three

Faith:
Its Purpose and Role in Our Life

*I*n addition to allowing the situation of your loved one's inactivity in the church to facilitate your spiritual growth, please be assured that there are other things that you can do. These include:

1. look to God when you hurt, and not focus on your circumstances
2. find or start a support group in your church to find encouragement, support and fellowship
3. be an encourager with and for your loved one whenever and **however** you are authentically prompted by the Holy Spirit

But most importantly of all, highlight the virtues of faith and prayer in your life. These virtues, in fact, will help you become more like Monica in your conviction that ultimately the grace of Christ will change hearts. Let's start, then, with some important aspects of faith.

As you know, God is constantly revealing Himself to us through the everyday people and circumstances that come into our lives. Our **response** to this on-going revelation is faith. Catechism of the Catholic Church, paragraph 143, states that "by faith, man completely submits his intellect and his will to God." So, faith is a personal adherence of the whole person to God (Catechism of the Catholic Church, paragraph 176). Additionally, faith has a twofold reference to the person of Christ, and to the truth (Catechism of the

Catholic Church, paragraph 177) that He proclaimed.

How does one get this faith? It's a gift from God. This gift, however, is given to all, but what is done with this gift of faith is up to the individual. God loves us so deeply that we can use His graces in whatever way we select. Please remember, though, that God wants to share His life with us. Ultimately, this is what will make us happy in this life and in the life to come. God wants us to experience His love, to deepen our relationship with Him, to share His life and His love with others as He asks us.

Let us pause here, early in our discussion of faith, to try a little exercise which I hope you will find helpful. This exercise has four parts:

1. Take a minute or two to think of someone who has made a real positive, difference in your life.
2. List (or mention to others) characteristics of the person who has made this positive difference.
3. Write out (or mention to others) what had to be true in order for this life-changing difference to have taken place. (After all, although this individual has been a great blessing to you, not everyone has experienced this person in the same way you have.)
4. Did this life changing difference take place all at once or did this change come about gradually?

Although this type of "faith analogy" is limited and therefore incomplete, I think it's a fair starting point. God reveals His loving presence to all, every day. We, in turn, need to be **open** to and **aware** of this presence. So much so that we are able, with God's grace, to look beyond what is, to see and experience the presence of God. Of course, this does not take place all at once, but gradually. In fact, God is constantly calling us deeper into relationship with Him, so that we will experience His peace and joy. And so God can use us in His world, with His people, and with the rest of His creation.

Abraham is called the father of all those who believe. Why? As an astute Israelite he could see the hand of God in most events that happened around him. He could see God's role in the process of delivering his people from the slavery of Egypt. He could see the action of God over and over in the history of his people and in his own life.

The prophet Jeremiah stood before the window of a potter's place and heard God say: "I am the potter, you are the clay." Today do we stand in front of the same window and see only the clay and the human potter?

The prophet Ezechiel carried on long, reflective discussions with the Lord. Fruitful deeds flowed from his life. As the Lord became more and more influential in his life, and as the Lord's power flowed through his life, this only deepened Ezechiel's trust and faith in God.

Let's take our earlier activity and apply it at a deeper level. Again, we'll use four steps.

1. Select **any** person or any event who/which has taken place in or touched your life today.
2. Look for a deeper meaning in that event or person through private reflection and prayer.
3. Reflect on this person or event in light of God's word.
4. Follow and act upon the movement of the Holy Spirit.

Your faith needs to be affirmed. You may have been raised in an age when you thought that the one group who would always have the right answers was the Church. At the same time, you might have thought that the one group that would never change would be the Church. But the Church itself depends totally on God. Our faith, therefore, is not primarily based on our knowledge of the teachings of Catholicism. Our faith is focused primarily on a person, and His name is Jesus. This has some very important and very practical dimensions to it. Many Catholics, when they think of Jesus present in our lives, think of the Eucharist. The Eucharist which was the real presence of Christ in the early Church is the same Eucharist that we share today. When St. Augustine reflected on the Eucharist with the people of his diocese, he said:

"Be what you see
See what you are."

We are all a very important element of Christ's Body. Turning to Christ in faith, in the Eucharist, is central to our lives as Catholics. Although we may be disappointed with our family members who have turned away from the Eucharist, we must love them and remain full of our faith. Our love and our faith will be the foundation for a deepening of our spiritual life. I'll close this section with one final reflection on faith.

Characteristically, we tend to divide human beings into two groups: true believers and unbelievers. A psychiatrist that I studied with in the early days of my ministry taught about these two basic types: those who live in their head and those who live in their gut. In religious language, we say that there are people who are by nature, affirmative. They see the positive side of life. On the other hand, there are people who are naturally skeptical and doubtful. I have seen this radical dichotomy when I do premarital counseling, but only rarely is the dichotomy as radical as it looks. However, people do have tendencies in one direction or the other. Yet, most of us

So true [handwritten margin note]

are probably represented best by the father who brings his epilepsy-stricken boy to Jesus (Jn 4:43-54). Jesus says to the man, "If you can believe, all things are possible to him who believes." The man replies, "<u>Lord, I believe, help my unbe-</u> <u>lief.</u>" Most of us are represented by that statement. We are *my mantra* believing unbelievers.

Especially in these days of mistrust in politics and business, we appreciate the importance of belief. With all the talk about family values we have had our views sharpened; most have not lost their appreciation for the importance of ideals. I remain impressed with the average citizen who knows that there are solid foundations on which s/he stands. I admire those who have gone through hard times and have demonstrated their belief in themselves. Yet, for most of us, there is a sense that our belief has been infiltrated with a persistent, gnawing unbelief.

There are good reasons for our unbelief. <u>We live in an age of unbelief.</u> I don't mean this observation as a criticism; it is simply a fact. People often ask me why our time has so little faith. Alfred North Whitehead, the great philosopher, pointed to one of the reasons for our present difficulty in believing. He made it clear that until the year 1800 humankind's way of living changed very little. Napoleon's ships, he pointed out, sailed at the same rate as those of Alexander the Great. But since 1800 travel speed has increased, scientific knowledge has increased and medical knowledge has increased. Everywhere we look there is change. The familiar cultural and social landmarks are gone.

We need only to look at ourselves to see a cause for our unbelief. We are working harder at living than we ever had to. There seems to be a general fatigue in the land. Perhaps we are spiritually fatigued. Moreover, the future seems very uncertain.

There is something I'd like to suggest for those of us who are believers but bothered by unbeliefs. If I may put this in the Catholic context, I have met many people who want to believe more deeply in God. They ask questions about the Trinity. I respond by saying not to begin with sophisticated doctrines. Begin with the notion that some greater power brought life to us. Reduce God to the simplest ideas. I say similar things to longstanding church people who want to believe more deeply in Our Lord. I respond by saying not to concentrate on the complex doctrine of the two natures of Christ. Begin simply with the fact of the moral character of Jesus. Reduce his life to something that makes simple sense. Much the same process applies to life after death. Begin with the notion that in the world of physics there is a basic conservation of energy. Nothing is ever lost. That is a simple notion leading to basic confidence, a confidence in God and in oneself. After all, you are a Catholic who has opened yourself to God and who continues to permit God to work through you. You forgive because God forgives you. You affirm the good in life, because division is contrary to God's will. You love and affirm all, because Christ died for all. You care, because God cares.

Chapter Four

Prayer

Paragaraph 2559 of the Catechism of the Catholic Church tells us that: "Prayer is the raising of one's mind and heart to God or the requesting of good things from God."[8] But when we pray, do we speak from the height of our pride and will, or "out of the depths" of a humble and contrite heart?[9] He who humbles himself will be exalted; humility is the foundation of prayer. Only when we humbly acknowledge that "we do not know how to pray as we ought"[10] are we ready to receive freely the gift of prayer. "Man is a beggar before God."[11]

To pray is to recognize our total dependence upon God for all that is good, every moment of every day. Another dimension of prayer is to listen to God speak to you of His deep, personal love for you. A third aspect of prayer is to allow God to assist us in seeing all of life from God's perspective (and not our perspective). Remember that Our Lord wants more than anything else an ever-deepening relationship with us. Therefore, in and through everything that is taking place in our lives, God is calling us ever more deeply to Himself. The good news of this is that we experience God's loving presence more deeply in our lives. Also, we open ourselves to permit God to work through us more clearly. Finally, we sense God's fingerprints on all that is going on in our lives. This brings us a stronger sense of God's peace. Let's continue, then, to take a more personal and more in-depth look at prayer.

I need to read this over and over and over and over

Recall that God speaks to us in our deepest experiences, feelings, desires, thoughts and ideas. So to be aware of our experiences is to become aware of God's work in them and then to offer ourselves completely to God **through** them.

Intimacy, then, is not primarily a sharing with another. Intimacy starts with being intimate with oneself. Intimacy is knowing the core of things myself.

For example, let's suppose someone I love has bursitis of the shoulder. Where is that person most present? Of course, where the bursitis is. The pain is intense. When I think of that person, what do I think of? I wonder, "How is the bursitis?" Wherever we are most present, God is most present. This is the importance of listening to where we are, and to listening well to all that is going on in our lives in the presence of God.

In prayer, then, we discover what we already have. Prayer helps us to experience what we already possess. Ignatius of Antioch, around A.D. 200, said, "The glory of God is the person fully alive." The more self-awareness we have, the more alive we become. This is what the Scripture means where it is recorded "The Reign of God is within" (Mk 9:1; Mt 16:18; 18:17).

God creates people with inherent value. So no mistake, failure, loss of image, exaggerated thinking or hurtful comments by others can take away or destroy this reality. We must stubbornly hold onto this fact of faith each day for ourselves, for others, and in gratitude for being made in God's image. In adopting this psychologically healthy way of thinking, we make an important spiritual statement of faith to ourselves and the world each day: my identity and value come from being a creation of God, and from nowhere else.

People who know their true selves and their true identity are at peace, and always have something to share with others – no matter how difficult the situation turns out to be. They are alive and those who encounter them enjoy the possibility of living more meaningful lives because of the gentle space they can offer them. People who know they are loved by God and gifted by God are grateful to God and seek to nurture these talents in themselves, and are in a fine position to be a spiritual and emotional oasis for a worried, anxious and depressed world. They have let go of an over-concern with personal image.

When people ask "Where is God in my life?" the best response I can give is "Where are **you**?" – that is where God is. In this way, prayer can be very practical and steeped in where we live. Prayer isn't "**come** as you are"; it's just **be** who you are.

A wonderful way to close each day is to "re-read" it. By going over all the things in that day that made me laugh, cry, sad, angry, joyful, etc. and to do it conscious of being in God's presence. Our hearts are like putty; if you work with putty it stays soft; if you don't, it becomes hard and impossible to move. By quietly going over the events of a day, we keep our hearts soft, our minds aware and our vision open to the presence of others, and of the Lord.

 Some important questions about myself and God to bring to prayer include:

  – What is holding me back from becoming a more loving person?
  – What has been my spirit, my mood during this past week?
  – Have anyone's words hit me more strongly than

usual?
- On a scale of 1 to 10, how happy am I?
- Do I feel called to do or let go of anything in my life?
- What discourages me? buoys me up? preoccupies me?
- Do I tend to be someone who frets and worries, or am I able to let things go in trust?
- Do I tend to control people and things?
- How do I handle worry?
- How do I handle conflict or differences with others?
- What situation would I most like to change in my life, but can't?
- Which answers to the questions above reveal those of a person of faith and prayer? Which answers lead me to look for God's love more deeply within myself so as to permit God's vision of life and God's thoughts and deeds to stream through me?

When you're feeling like you need a real "pick-me-up," don't listen to any negative thoughts inside you, but instead:

1. stop, sit down in spite of your hesitant or discouraged feelings
2. quiet yourself by closing your eyes
3. recite a short prayer
4. open your eyes and read a few verses of a helpful Scripture passage or a few lines from a book you've found to be a good companion presently or in the past
5. slowly and with a gentle respect think about these words from Scripture or the text you've selected

It is not what we say about prayer that matters. What

matters is what we do. I'd like to make a brief notation about the particular relevance of quiet morning prayer for those of us who would seek to be a caring presence in the world. To be involved with God the first thing each day centers us on what is important. In addition, it helps us to be awake to the day stretching out before us. And, too, morning silence and solitude can better enable us to come to our senses and be in the **now**. This is especially important so we don't miss those interpersonal encounters that might bring us closer to God if we weren't nostalgically reflecting on the past or preoccupied with the future.

It may be helpful for you to check your balance concerning these:

1. stimulation and quiet
2. reflection and action
3. work and leisure
4. self-care and care of others
5. self-improvement and patience
6. future aspirations and present realities
7. involvement and detachment

We pray because we remember that moments of grace spread like waves all through our lives. God arrives when we are not looking, touches us when our backs are turned. God comes:

   – in the arms of a friend who loves me despite my faults;

   – in a telephone call from someone who's in pain;

   – in the voice of someone calling you "sweetie."

Our prayer, then, lies in remembering those moments to discover the One who has been and is present. For us to be faithful to daily, private prayer is to be faithful to our lives. To be faithful to daily prayer is never to let life become "just one damn thing after another," but to savor each moment's richness, feel each moment's pain, acknowledge its tedium, and celebrate its love. Prayer is letting God love me. God does. My task is to notice, to remember and to stake my life on those truths.

Let's situate our day, contextualize it a bit. The book of Ecclesiastes says that there is a time for everything. A time to be "wasted" is necessary every day. Father Henri Nouwen once told a story about a carpenter and an apprentice. They went to the woods where the apprentice asked: "Why has this tree never been cut down and used to make things?" The reason, said the carpenter, was that it was useless. And so we'll just let it grow and be itself, and allow people to find detachment here, and rest, and shade. This day could be used for lots of other important things, but our **need** is for the Lord to speak to us.

Look around us – because there is a creation, there must be a Creator. But why have creation? What could creatures give God that God doesn't already have? This question leads us into the only motivation that makes creation make sense – love. So don't pray because of some obligation or some nice idea. Pray to know again and again how deeply loved you are by the giver of all life. God loves you and indeed has intentions for what will become of this life of yours. So we pray first, to be reminded of God and God's love, and second, to want this life of God and this will of God to be more deeply **our** life and **our** will. The conviction of faith for the Catholic is that I can give God to people as no one else can. The presence is based on an exchange between me and the one I am serving. How I live out my Christianity is based primarily upon my relationship with God. If it is **strong**, then my relationship with others will be strong, healthy and helpful. We pray so as to keep these thoughts in mind so that we never lose sight of what life is all about, that is, God's love and grace and its importance in the lives of everyone we meet. To have that vitality and that fidelity, we have to **want** this life for ourselves and for all others. And what keeps us growing in God's life, despite all of the distasteful things that happen is that the life of God, God's peace and love, are worth it! And we know that this conviction comes to us and grows gradually, not all at once. We must keep at it daily, often, through prayer.

Let **us** now think very interiorly about these thoughts. Are **we** the person God has called **us** to be? Let's go back and rediscover three people to assist **us**, perhaps, in the ongoing process of discovering ourselves before God. Remember: God's call to each one of us continues each day. God's call is going out right now. It's personal and it's touching. Why? To help us deepen our conviction and confidence.

Person One: Moses in the Book of Exodus. Moses is seen as a very strong person interiorly. He is very clear about the meaning and direction of his life. God says the misery of the Israelites is understood and calls Moses to deliver them. But Moses asks God: "Who am I to do such a thing?" and tells God: "No." But God is very patient, and asks Moses again, only to receive a second "No." Eventually God gets Aaron to go with Moses, and Moses still dodges the call until God says it is **you** I want, Moses, I know you and what you're made of, your problems and weaknesses. I know what I need from you.

Person Two: Jeremiah in chapter one. The Lord tells Jeremiah, "Before you were in your mother's womb, I knew you." Although he accepts God's call, Jeremiah knows his mission will be difficult. So, in his life he argues with Yahweh; telling God, "You seduced me." He knew that some people were not open to hearing the word of God. Jeremiah was not anxious to plunge into God's life, which calls for self-denial and doing the right thing, even if it is not the popular option. The good news is that like Moses, Jeremiah did respond to the Lord's call and both men were towers of strength.

Person Three: 2 Samuel, chapter three. The key question raised in this chapter in the dialogue between Samuel and Eli, is where is the call coming from? There was the issue of discernment concerning to whom and to what Samuel was called. Samuel was human. He had his virtues and his faults, like each of us. Samuel was young, open and receptive. Because of these qualities of openness and receptiveness, God was able to use him, despite his faults.

Are you receptive to this call of God that is addressed to you, each moment, each day?

Don't ever allow anyone or anything to distract you from what your mission really is: namely, sharing God's life and love, and your fervent desire to want it more and more in you and in others. As we read in Psalm 40: "In your will is my delight."

Do you look for, and see, Christ in the difficult people and events in your life? Do you look for, and see, Christ in the unexpected situations that arise? Do you act as if you trust God to be involved in everything that is happening, and will happen?

Prayer as listening to God

Another reason to stop and listen in prayer: Often, people will feel sad or lonely when they become task-oriented, even when the task is a mission-oriented church activity. It is not at all uncommon to hear people say, "I throw/threw myself into my work or job." At these times it is important to stop and to ask: what does this mean? Sometimes, in service-oriented individuals, after awhile, people will take you and your service for granted. People stop orally or tangibly rewarding you. Do you become dissatisfied and resentful when this happens?

Often, if this is the case, you'll want to do more and more (activity) to get people to pay attention. But if you have a strong need for recognition, you'll never get enough satisfaction, no matter how you perform. This is particularly sad because it goes right back to the heart of "why pray?" again. Pray so as to keep yourself aware of how deeply loved you are by God and, therefore, what a great person you are. I'd like to suggest to you that at least three times every day, you offer the ejaculation "I am fearfully and wonderfully made." This is true because God loves you. In fact, there is no one in the world that God loves more than you right now! Therefore, teach, guide, parent, counsel, etc. whatever you do, because you enjoy doing God's will for you at this time in your life! You must trust God enough and love yourselves enough so that you exist not for tasks and/or praise, but for God. Honestly now:

a) What do you think of yourself?

b) Do you work on a "performance" basis?

c) How do you feel when the applause for you stops?

Remember, love yourself. You'll always have you and God. Remember, too, that it takes great heroism to devote one's life to others in a situation which is frustrating and unsatisfactory, and in which one's sacrifice may even be, in large measure, wasted. But here above all, faith in God is necessary. God sees our sacrifice and will make it fruitful. This is so even though in our own eyes there is nothing apparent but futility and frustration. When we accept this grace, our eyes are opened to see the real, unsuspected good in others, and we become truly grateful for our Christian vocation.

A final theme on prayer that I would like to discuss with you is that prayer enhances the world. Look at Psalm 42. It expresses the desire for God's presence in our lives. Furthermore, it speaks of a real desire for the experience of God. Matthew 6:19 is also a wonderful verse for meditating on how we view ourselves and how we view God. Where do you put your own heart?

Everything in reality exists in God's mind. Things are real because God knows them, not vice versa. God loves what is real, and therefore we exist. God loves creation into existence. God knows it and loves it, and therefore it's real. One's whole existence depends on this. People are lovable and magnificent and real, by God's design. We must accept this on faith.

John 14:1-14 tells the story of the Last Supper. Here, Our Lord speaks of Himself as drawing all to God. In prayer, we want to grow in the knowledge of ourselves that God has. This takes real honesty (to know ourselves as we truly are). We are creatures with real limits, and without God's presence, we are nothing. No one person on earth can carry or contain God's fullness. We need each other. We must allow others to make God's presence known to us. We can block God's presence from coming across to others if we ever forget who we are, or what we're called to do. It's the presence of God in each of us that makes people lovable.

If we refuse to reflect carefully on what God wants us to

be, we can't be our real selves. God, who created us, has a plan for us. For God to fully live His life through us, we need to be constantly created and recreated in His image. For this to happen, we want to allow all of our life experiences to enter our daily private prayer. This is a real outpouring of all of yourself. The importance and significance of this is that more and more we see things in relation to God and from God's perspective, and not merely in relation to ourselves or our narrow perspective.

The world? Well, when St. Francis Xavier died on a small island off the coast of China four centuries ago, it took a few years before his superior, St. Ignatius Loyola, received the "news" of his death. Today, we often see things that are happening on far-away places on the day they take place. Do we pray for our deeply wounded world since we know so much more about it? You see, we have access to what's happening in the lives of people near and far almost right away. Our faith calls us to respond to the needs of people as God would have us. To be aware of this is important because faith falters when guilt replaces hope and shame dissolves solidarity, or when outrage consumes hope and hatred replaces love. Then our task to make disciples of nations degenerates into a sentimental dream with very little sense of mission.

I suspect that while we become more informed about the world, we become less transformed by the living Christ. The strategy of the power of evil is to make us think of life as a huge stack of very complicated issues; too complex to respond to; too frustrating to deal with. The more entangled we become in issues, the harder it is to recognize Jesus as the saving Lord of history.

As long as issues dominate our lives, we miss the essence

the crux of the matter (handwritten margin note)

of prayer. Prayer is not directed to, or at, issues. It is not meant to unravel complexities or solve problems. Prayer is directed to a personal God who loves us and hears us; it is a cry from heart to heart, from spirit to spirit.

Issues easily imprison us. A person (Jesus) can set us free. Issues easily divide us. A person can unite us. Issues easily exhaust. A person can give us rest. Issues easily destroy us. A person can offer new life. An orientation toward issues causes despair, but hope emerges when we direct ourselves to the person of a saving God. This is prayer.

Jesus leaves little doubt about the meaning of prayer when He says: "Apart from me you can do nothing. Those who dwell in me as I dwell in them, bear much fruit" (Jn 15:5). Dwelling in Jesus is what prayer is about. However, when our concern no longer flows from our personal encounter with the living Christ, we feel an oppressive weight.

However, there are critical issues Catholics **must** try to solve.

True prayer colors our outlook on everything in life. So, then, can we see Christ in the world? No, but serious and sincere efforts at daily prayer will gradually permit the God in us to see Christ's presence more clearly in all of the common, ordinary, everyday events and people of our life. Through our prayer, then, the God in us opens our eyes to Christ among us. This is what is meant by the expression, "Spirit speaks to spirit." Thus, Catholics who become involved in Central America, for example, do not move from prayer to politics, but from prayer to prayer. Apart from Jesus, the agonies of our world make us run away and hide. To pray, therefore, is to connect whatever human struggle or pain we encounter with the heart of Jesus.

So, then, how do we get started at prayer? Maybe the most helpful advice I can suggest to you is simply to take a few minutes every day to be silent. We all have plenty of opportunities to be silent. Taking a walk alone, sitting quietly before or after Mass, driving to the store. Be still and gently remind yourself that you are in the presence of God who loves you and wants to address you this day. Go as deeply into yourself as you can go and listen to God. We want to be sure to do this on a daily basis because prayer is not some action to be performed now and then. No, prayer is a way of life. Our prayer is to influence everything about our life. Prayer influences our way of looking at everything that happens in our life. It affects our "being," our level and depth of humanness in response to other people, things and the rest of creation. Our prayer is what permits us to carry in our heart all kinds of pain and human sorrow, all kinds of needs and desires. The good news is that prayer works.

But how do I distinguish what I want from what **God** wants for me. I'm reminded here of St. Ignatius' own instructions in the "Spiritual Exercises" where he encourages the retreatant to pray for that which s/he desires.

Praying through our desires helps us to live in faith. For we cannot know our own will, let alone God's, unless we get in touch with our own deepest desires.

All of us experience a deep longing and yearning for God. Whenever we sincerely respond to this longing we are also responding to the grace of God, who has planted this desire within us. And there is a point within our very being where the distinction between our own desires and God's desires somehow get blurred. One of my favorite lines is from Psalm

40, where David writes: "To do your will, O God, is my delight." Pay attention to the restlessness of your own heart. Pay attention to those interior desires. Pay attention ... maybe God is saying something to you there. God speaks to you through your experience. Listen with attentiveness and faith. The Almighty wishes to do great things to, and through, your life. A story on the role of prayer and the power of God may be helpful here.

Several years ago a young pediatric neurosurgeon was talking about a delicate brain surgery he had performed on a child who had been close to death. When he finished he said: "We've done all we can. Now it's up to God."

The quote was carried in all of the television and news-paper reports coming out of the Johns Hopkins Hospital at press conference. Reporters picked up on the statement about God.

Dr. Ben Carson, the surgeon, knows the role of prayer and the power of God in the midst of pain, suffering and misunderstanding. Raised in inner-city Detroit, Dr. Carson, a very poor black youngster, tells the story of himself as a crazy 14-year-old with a violent temper, who had just attempted to stab another teenager in the abdomen because, as he described it, "He made me angry." Fortunately, his intended victim's life was miraculously spared when the knife struck his large metal belt buckle and broke.

The 14-year-old Carson was terrified by what he had done because he realized he was completely out of control. Afterward he locked himself up in the bathroom for three hours, and in his desperation he turned to God, remembering what his mother would do in time of trouble.

He prayed and he said, "God, it's up to you. You must take this temper away from me." And he started reading the

Book of Proverbs. Dr. Carson has since remarked that he has read verses and chapters from that book each day because, he says, "It is just full of advice on how to live."

After that day, his life would change. He said he adopted God, his heavenly Father, as his earthly father, since he had grown up without a father. He said he began to feel that God was somebody you could talk to, somebody who would answer prayers and give you wisdom. And his relationship with God was a relationship that has grown.

Let's take another example from Scripture and see the power of God at work in response to one who believes and prays. In Matthew chapter 8, verses 5-13, we have a non-Jew, an atheist, a centurion, coming to Jesus and asking Him to work a miracle and we hear the words we say right before we receive Communion: "Lord, I am not worthy that you should enter under my roof." The significance of this centurion's faith lies in his trust that Jesus can perform the cure without appearing in person. It will be enough if Jesus utters just one single word of command.

And isn't that our situation today? We come to the Lord with many requests – we ask for all kinds of things – big and small. We too often go to the Lord, begging that a son or daughter will return to the Church, that a friend or relative be cured of cancer or recover from alcoholism, whatever. Some would argue: "Why should we ask God for something that He already knows that we need." After all, God knows our anguish as we think about our child missing Mass, or of the friend languishing in a hospital bed ... why bother? From the Gospel story, we see that Jesus can help us only if we first seek Him out in faith. There is a mysterious law in the world of prayer which is demonstrated in the Gospel, namely, that God, by His own decree, somehow places power in the hands

of persons like the centurion who come to the Lord inter-
ceeding in such a way that unless they intercede, the Lord's
power is withheld.

It is very important for us to continue to turn to God, not
only with our petitions, but with our very lives. The late
Indian Jesuit theologian Father Tony DeMello told this story
of a simple villager who lived with his wife and children and
worked to support his family. Each day, however, in addition
to his work, the villager made time for private devotions in
his parish church. As he left his house, he would stop in his
doorway, raise his hand in farewell and say, "Goodbye, Lord
God, I'm off to church now to perform my religious duties."

We can all appreciate the moral of that story: that God is
present everywhere, that we can pray everywhere, that wherever we find our deepest peace and our deepest anguish, we
are likely to find the Lord. And each of us has our own way
of allowing the Lord to be present to us throughout the day.
We may have a prayer that we like to say at work or in the
car. We may have some other devotion, some link to keep us
connected throughout the day to the source of our very
being. I recently read a beautiful prayer from Pope John
XXIII, who had his own way of keeping himself centered on
God. He once wrote:

I love to feel myself bound forever to you, Lord, with a
gold chain, woven of lovely delicate links –

The first link: Justice which obliges me to find God
wherever I turn.

The second link: The providence and goodness which
will guide my feet.

The third link: Love for my neighbor, unwearying and most patient.

The fourth link: The Sacrifice that must always be my lot, that I will and must welcome at all times.

The fifth link: The Glory that Jesus promises me in this life and in Eternity.

Prayer as communication and action

Sometimes a single word can enrich our lives for a day. Words still hold a great power over us, especially the spoken word. The ancients knew this. For them to know something's name was to have power over it. This is why Adam could name all the animals, but Jacob could not name the angel who wrestled with him. In the Old Testament, the word was called *dabar,* meaning something of great power and potency. The word was not merely an uttered syllable, but something of force. Isaiah said, "The word of God goes forth and will not return until it accomplishes its end."

It is difficult for us to remember that the word was long spoken before it was written. In the Middle Ages, most of the monks, like the general population, could not read. Every morning, however, they would meet in chapel in front of a large Bible. In silence they would listen, while a literate monk would read a single passage out loud. He would step back after this short reading, bow, and retire in silence. He would get up and read again the same passage. And this he did over and over again until the chapel was empty. The idea was that as each monk got something out of the reading to take with him during the day, he would leave. As the word penetrated his life, he was ready for life. The word has power.

How absolutely neat!

So, too, you may wish to start your day with a prayer of one word, be it "God," or "Jesus" or "love," or "hope." Fasten this word to your heart so that it never goes far from you. The word "Jesus" is an especially powerful word. Let that word be your shield. Carry it with you in prayer, observance, thought and action.

Our actions, too, can be a source of prayer. For example, there is the story of the traditional Hebrew tale about an old farmer who went out into his field. He worked in the field and then could not return to his home because it was the Sabbath. When he returned to his village, his Rabbi asked the old man: "Did you pray while you were in the field over the Sabbath?" The farmer looked at the Rabbi and said, "Rabbi, you know that I am not a learned man. You know that I do not know the Sacred Prayers. I could not pray while I was in the field." The Rabbi then asked, "What did you do through all those long hours while you were in the field over the Sacred Sabbath?" The old man said, "I could only recite the letters of the alphabet and ask God to form them into something that has meaning."

Each of us stands before God carrying with us the alphabet of our own experience. Our experiences are very different. During our lives, we go through so much. We experience success and failure, joy and sadness, friendship and isolation, love and rejection. We try so hard to make meaning of the good times and the hard times that we may be forced to endure. But maybe like the farmer, we can offer it all, the letters of the alphabet, to the Lord, and ask God to form them into something that has meaning.

Notice that the farmer recited all the letters, and relied on God to make sense out of what was of no sense to him. He trusted God to shape the meaning of his life. There is great consolation to be had here – offering to God **all that happens to us**, and ultimately letting God shape the meaning for us.

Our prayer and the Lord's prayer

We shouldn't end our reflections on prayer without taking a look at the Lord's Prayer itself. After all, it **is** the Lord's Prayer. Be careful: in Matthew 6, Jesus says, "Your Father knows what you need before you ask Him. ..." When the disciples asked Jesus to teach them to pray, he told them to say one Our Father. Looking at St. Luke's version of the Our Father, we see that every one of these phrases is a petition. It may be good to imagine for a moment hearing Jesus say these very words to you. Ask yourself: "Do I really believe those words? What sense do they make to me?"

Of course we are all very familiar with the Lord's Prayer. It's the one prayer that everybody knows. Sometimes it becomes a prayer formula that we simply repeat. But there is, in effect, the heart of the most basic teaching Jesus gave to His apostles. The Lord's Prayer is a school of prayer. It articulates the deepest desires and aspirations that flow out of the human spirit.

Desire is an enormously complex word. In spirituality, we talk about "holy" desires. These are desires which orient a person toward God and which are considered, therefore, to be graces from God. In competitive athletics, we hear men and women speak about the "spark of desire" which transforms a mediocre team or performer into a champion. In our schools, we promote the desire for excellence. We also speak of desires for love, for companionship, for meaning, and the like.

Desires are powerful. Desires give strong and energetic orientation to the psyche. St. Ignatius was a man of great and intense desires. At the time of his conversion, he indulged in an exercise that can best be termed holy daydreaming by means of which he could see himself in fantasy undertaking great and difficult enterprises for God. He would recall the great exploits of the saints and say to himself: "St. Francis did such and such for the Lord. I shall do more. St. Dominic did these great deeds for the Lord. I shall do more." He tells us that this holy exercise always left him with a feeling of peace and devotion and strength that he later termed spiritual consolation.

This makes good psychological sense. <u>You can hardly achieve what you cannot even see in imagination. You must be a man or woman of great desires and great vision if you are going to say "Thy Kingdom come, Thy will be done, on earth</u> as it is in heaven."

You will note that when Jesus was asked by his disciples to teach them to pray, He taught them to say "Father in Heaven, Hallowed be your name." He begins with His Father, with His Father's Kingdom, His Father's interests. Jesus was primarily a man whose desires were oriented toward doing His Father's will. His desires were God-centered. So, too, our desires must be God-centered. We have to be careful that we can sort out those desires that will lead us close to God from those desires which come from outside, from television and advertising in particular, where we find consumer items, status, and even a secure brand of happiness all packaged, presented and peddled as desirables.

The toughest part of the Lord's Prayer may be "Thy will be done." This is the God-centered part of our desires. It is sometimes difficult to pray that I ask not that my will be done but that the will of God will be done. The supreme test of faith is to pray with belief that God wills what is ultimately good and profitable for us from the vantage point of our eternal well-being.

It is probably only at the end of the world that we shall realize how the destinies of persons and nations have been shaped, not so much by the external actions of powerful men and women, or by events that seemed inevitable, but by the quiet, silent, irresistible prayer of persons the world will never know. Let us pray with the same confidence, <u>asking God that our deepest desires and yearnings</u> find their home with God.

Prayer as contemplation

Another important facet of prayer is contemplation. One definition of contemplation states that <u>contemplation is a long, loving look at the real.</u> Each word in the definition is crucial: long – loving – look – at the real.

First, the real. Reality is living, pulsing people. Reality is fire and water. Reality is a child lapping a chocolate ice cream cone. Reality is Christ Jesus.

I look at this real. I do not analyze it, or describe it, or even define it. No, instead I am one with it. I do not move around with it. I enter it. But this long look at the real must be a loving look. It demands that the real delights me, captivates me. We see that in the Gospel story of Martha and Mary that Mary is described sitting at Christ's feet totally immersed in Him, and so she contemplates His words. And isn't that what prayer is? Contemplating Christ. Taking a long, loving look at Him. Contemplation calls forth love, pleasure, even delight. Contemplation is not study or cold examination. It is not a computer operation. Rather, to contemplate is to be in love.

You can study things, even people, but unless you enter into this intuitive communion with them, you can only know about them; you don't know them really. To take a long look at something, be it a child, a glass of wine, a beautiful meal, a loved one, this is indeed a natural act of contemplation. This is something that takes practice. There's the nub. All the way through school, we are taught to abstract. We are not taught loving awareness.

Mary sat at the Lord's feet and listened resolutely to His word. Martha, on the other hand, was drawn here and there, full of anxiety to get the table set. Jesus was honored by Martha's active love in serving Him. But more so by Mary who listened to His words so carefully, so contemplatively. Jesus lays down the principle that listening to His words is the one thing necessary. This is primary. Not that waiting on table and all other works of charity are unimportant. However, they must never prevent a person from first listening to the word of God.

To contemplate the word of God in prayer is to listen, to pay attention, to take a long, loving look at the real, to look at Christ.

From contemplation comes communion. By that I mean the discovery of the holy, the deep thoughtful encounters, where love is proven by sacrifice, the exchange of all else for God. But how do we realize this capacity for contemplation this oneness with God? One basic suggestion is to read. To make friends with remarkable men and women who have themselves looked long and lovingly at the real. The list is long and impressive: people like Matthew, Mark, Luke and John, Teresa of Avila and Mother Teresa.

Contemplation is our ageless tradition. It goes back to Jesus alone with His Father on the mountain, in the desert, in the garden. It goes back to the early Fathers of the Church, to medieval mystics, to Aquinas, to John of the Cross. Not to contemplate is to betray our tradition. So many of the contemplatives in the past sensed one basic truth, namely, that our activity will be fruitless unless we are men and women of prayer.

The world is thirsty for men and women who know and love God intimately. Only such men and women can witness to the living God that these times demand. Contemplation is the mark of a lover of God. When we pray for another or when we pray with another, it is important to think about the words we use and to whom they are directed. Words without thoughts never go to heaven.

Prayer as petition

Many people shy away from prayer because they are afraid that God won't answer their requests. This, of course, casts doubt on their own belief in God. Other people boast of their own success in having their prayers answered. But invariably, success in prayer does not prove the Christian doctrine that "whatever you ask for in my name I will give you." That would prove, instead, something more like magic, some kind of power in certain people to control or compel the course of nature.

The Gospel seems to impress upon us that persevering prayer will not remain unheard. God will hear prayer without delay. But we know too, that not all prayers are immediately answered, for in the very heart of the Gospel we meet a glaring instance to the contrary. In Gethsemane, the holiest of all petitioners, Our Lord Himself, prayed three times that a certain cup might pass from Him. And that cup did not pass.

The English writer, C.S. Lewis, once commented on this notion of prayer. He had remarked that he had seen it suggested that a team of people should agree to pray as hard as they knew how, over a period of six weeks, for all of the patients in Hospital A, and to pray for none of those in Hospital B. Then someone would tally up the results to see if "A" had more cures and fewer deaths. Of course the experiment was doomed from the start because those praying were doing so, not to alleviate the patients' sufferings, but rather to test God's ways. Empirical proofs as to the efficacy of prayer are unobtainable.

But the conclusion will seem less depressing if we remember that prayer is a request, and should be compared with examples of the same thing. We make requests of our friends, family and business associates all the time. We ask for a pay raise or ask a friend to feed the dog while we are away or even ask our children to clean up their rooms. Sometimes we get what we ask for, sometimes not. Whatever we obtain after requesting it, we might have gotten anyway. Possibly our boss or our friend or children may tell us that they acted because we asked. And we know them so well we feel sure, first, that they are saying what they believe to be true, and secondly that they understand their own motives well enough to be right. But notice, our assurance is based on the relationship we have with these people. So too with God. Our assurance that God always hears and sometimes grants our prayer can come in the same way.

Prayer and our disposition before God

Another important insight into prayer is offered to us in the Gospel story of the tax collector and the Pharisee in the Temple. Both of these men prayed. Both were convinced of the truth of what they said in their prayers. What the Pharisee said was an accurate reflection of his deepest disposition. The thanks that he offered God revealed his self righteousness and the contempt he felt for others. By describing himself as a Pharisee, he was proudly claiming to be separated and apart from the others.

As a sinner, the tax collector, too, is separated. Virtuous Jews avoided him and excluded him from their company. The tax collector was standing at a distance. He did not deserve to stand among good people. And his prayer only had a few words to it. He prayed simply that God would be merciful to him a sinner.

We find ourselves being called to compare Pharisee and tax collector, and to ask ourselves who is the just one in God's eyes? Who is the good one, and who really is the bad one in this story?

The Pharisee was scrupulously exact in fulfilling the many difficult precepts of the law. The tax collector, on the other hand, was dishonest. He collaborated with the enemies of his own people. And Jesus knew what his listeners thought and the judgment he proclaimed was in direct contrast to theirs.

Moving the parable from Palestine to our own turf, what does it say to us? After all, Luke didn't write the Gospel only for the Jews of Jesus' time. The parables of Jesus are not sheer history. They are our parables.

And this parable, in particular, challenges us to look at

our own moral consciousness, how we compare ourselves with others, how we measure up morally. Perhaps we are not so blatant as the Pharisee is portrayed. None of us would be so bold as to pray: "Thank you, God, that I am not like the rest of humankind." That would be too much even for the most arrogant. But throughout history, men and women have fallen prey, in some measure, to the Pharisee's fault. Early Christians looked down on Jews as "rejected by God." Crusaders looked down on non-believers in Christ, whom they would massacre. Protestants and Catholics in Northern Ireland despise one another. Upper classes look down on lower classes.

As we see with the Pharisee, a well developed conscience does not translate, necessarily, into a morally courageous life. Talking about moral decision-making in his book titled "The Moral Life of Children," Robert Coles, the noted Harvard child psychiatrist, makes some interesting observations on this subject. He writes of being helped in the effort at moral clarification by a poor African American woman in New Orleans, whom he met in the early 1960s during the period when the schools were being integrated there. This woman observed, "There's a lot of people who talk about doing good, and a lot of people who argue about what's good and what's not good." And she added, "There are some folks who just put their lives on the line for what's right, and they may not be the ones who talk a lot or argue a lot for what's right, they just do a lot."

The woman's daughter happened to be Ruby Bridges, one of the black children who at age six, initiated school desegration in New Orleans against terrible and fearful odds. For days that turned into weeks, and weeks that turned into months, this child had to brave murderously heckling mobs, hurling threats and slurs and hysterical denunciations and accusations as she traveled to and from school in the morning and evening. Federal marshalls took her to school and brought her home every day. For a good part of the year, she attended school all by herself, owing to a total boycott by white families.

But still Ruby persisted, and so did her parents. Ruby's teachers began to wonder how long she could take it. One teacher related how one day she saw Ruby coming down the street with the federal marshalls on both sides of her. The crowd was there shouting as usual. A woman spat at Ruby, but missed. Ruby smiled at her. A man shook his fist at her. Ruby smiled at him. Then she walked up the stairs and stopped and turned and smiled one more time. And you know what she told one of the marshalls? She told him she prayed for those people, the ones in the mob, every night before she went to sleep.

When asked about those prayers for the people who had been so unswervingly nasty to her, she replied, "I go to church every Sunday, and we're told to pray for everyone, even the bad people, and so I do." She had no more to say on that score.

The Gospel challenges us to ponder on what conditions Christ's coming will bring salvation? Who will be able to stand his ground on judgment day? Who will enter the Kingdom of God in its final state? Will the Pharisee be there? The tax collector? Ruby Bridges? Members of the mob who threatened her? You? Me?

Maybe Ruby Bridges herself will have the final say on this one, as to who will be ultimately saved. In one interview with

Robert Coles she explained: "They keep coming and saying bad words, but my momma says that they'll get tired after a while and they'll stop coming. They'll stay home. The minister came to our house and he said the same thing; not to worry, and I don't. The minister says God is watching and He won't forget, because He never does. The minister says if I forgive the people and smile at them, God will keep a good eye on everything, and He'll be our protection."

And so we pray for the grace to be humble. And we pray for the grace to be forgiving. And we pray that the Lord will hear our prayer for mercy.

Prayer as intercession

Another key element of prayer is intercessory prayer. How often have you told someone that you would pray for them? Intercessory prayer, or prayer for others, can be quite powerful, and I believe that God calls people to pray for others in a very special way.

Most of the time when we pray for others, we are praying that this suffering is alleviated, or that this sorrow be lifted, or that a solution be found to a problem. And in many cases, praying for others becomes a last resort, when all else fails.

I have found that the more I pray for others, the more I forget my own needs and problems. Compassion really lies at the heart of our prayer for our fellow human beings. And isn't that an important message of the Gospel? One definition of compassion is the sometimes fatal capacity for feeling what it is like to live inside somebody else's skin. It is the knowledge that there can never really be any peace and joy for me, until there is peace and joy finally for you.

But in the end, compassion is not yours or mine, but God's gift to us. And in praying for others we find God holding us in a compassionate embrace.

Praying for our wants and our hurts

One more comment on prayer. There is a story that the Chinese tell of an old man who owned a bony plow-horse. One spring afternoon the horse ran away, and the old man's friends, trying to console him said, "We're so sorry about your horse, old man. What a misfortune you've had." But the old man said, "Bad news, good news, who knows?" A few days later the horse returned home, leading a herd of wild horses. Again the friends came running. Filled with jubilation, they cried, "How wonderful!" But the old man whispered, "Good news, bad news, who knows?" Then the next day, when the farmer's son was trying to ride one of the new horses, he was thrown to the ground and broke both his legs. The friends gasped. The old man stood still and said, "Bad news, good news, who knows?" And a short time later when the village went to war and the young men were drafted to fight, the farmer's son was excused because of two broken legs. "Good news, bad news, who knows?"

Things happen to us. We can't always figure them out. Good news? Bad news? Often times we don't get what we prayed for and we can't understand what God has in mind. Sometimes we feel God has let us down when we needed God the most. We begin to analyze the situation. We try to rationalize why God did not give us what we prayed for. We say, "You didn't get what you prayed for because you didn't deserve it." Or, "You didn't get what you prayed for because God knows what is best for you, even better than you do." Or, "You didn't get what you prayed for because someone else's prayer for the opposite was more worthy." Or, maybe you didn't get what you prayed for because prayer "is a sham." "God doesn't hear our prayers. Because there is no God..." Good news? Bad news?

It all depends on your perspective. Have you ever heard a man or woman of God say that God has failed them? I haven't. That's the good news!

Recognize that the suffering that you are enduring because your son/daughter is not going to Mass, which is so much a part of your life right now, can be the catalyst for you to carry forth the healing ministry of Christ through the church in many ways.

Reflection Questions:

1. Do you believe you are called to grow closer to God? How do you know this?

2. What is the role of prayer in your life right now? In light of what has been suggested, how might your prayer life change?

3. How does your own life experience, including suffering, equip you to experience Our Lord's presence, and also to carry on His healing ministry?

4. What changes are needed to make you more aware of Christ's presence in your everyday life? How do you see your response to Christ's presence as a gift to your family members, to the church, and even to the world?

A Prayer

God of love and mercy
You call us
to be your people,
You fill us with
Your abundant grace.
Make us a holy people,
radiating the fullness
of your love.
Form us into a community,
a people who care,
expressing your compassion.
Remind us day after day
of our baptismal call to serve with joy and courage.
Teach us how to grow in wisdom and grace and
joy in Your presence.
Through Jesus Christ and in your Spirit,
we make this prayer.

Chapter Five

Pastoral Issues and Responses

QUESTION: Am I a bad parent because my son/daughter is not going to Mass regularly?

RESPONSE: No, absolutely not. If we read the chapters of the Book of Genesis, we hear God say that God looked at all creation and said it was good. In fact, you are so **good** that you are made in the image and likeness of God. You are so worthwhile that Jesus would have suffered, died and risen for you, if you were the only person on earth. Your goodness doesn't flow from what you **do.** Your goodness flows from who you are, namely, a child of God. Nevertheless, it **may** be the case that the parent failed in certain responsibilities. Repenting of that, if it occurred, is important. But just asking the question indicates the desire to be a good parent.

QUESTION: Am I responsible for my child's actions?

RESPONSE: There is a very important and extremely practical distinction between being responsibile "for" another, and being responsible "to" another. Every human being is responsible "to" every other human being whose life we are privileged to touch. Whether we like it or not, whether we realize it or not, our thoughts, words, attitudes and dispositions will have an impact on others, for the good or the "not so good." However, what another person does with our love, goodness, caring, etc., is out of our hands. We cannot make another person love us or love God. In fact, one of the toughest aspects of love is to truly love another and then to "let go," knowing and trusting that love always sets the other free to respond in whatever way "the other" desires to respond. The other person is responsible "for" their actions. In short, then, I'm always responsible "to" another adult. I'm never responsible "for" that adult.

(Love others, then let go, and leave them in the best hands possible, the hands of God.)

QUESTION: Did my child lose the faith?

RESPONSE: This is a loaded question, but let me do my best to answer it briefly.

First of all, "lose" is the wrong word because it suggests it involved no act of the will.

Second, the spiritual training of children includes:

1. teaching the truths of the faith
2. modeling the truths of the faith
3. taking the God-given right to tell a child what to believe and acting on it.

We take our right as parents to be the primary religious educator of our children from the teachings of the Church, from the Scriptures and from the Creator, who continues in the life-giving act of creation including instructions on right and wrong.

God commanded parents to train their children in the way they should go, and God promised that, if we do our jobs as well as we can, then when the child is old that s/he will not depart from it. Or, at least the probabilities are that the child will have this foundation throughout life. So, parents have a **right** and an **obligation** to train their children spiritually, and it comes from God.

If a parent remains neutral in this area, there is a high degree of probability that the child will grow up to reject God. This is so because the child will model what the parents have shown him/her in these matters.

Even if a parent has put forth his or her best efforts in this area, however, remember, none of us can give faith to another. Faith is God's gift to us. A child may imitate the actions of parents at Mass, for example, but over time, the child must gradually internalize the meaning and significance of faith in everyday life. I can't lose something I've never had. Faith is always a matter of both depth and degree. I always want, with God's help, to be in an ongoing process of becoming a deeper believer, more complete believer, more devout believer, particularly in terms of my relationship with Our Lord.

QUESTION: What about the role of guilt?

RESPONSE: We can say that guilt is that inner experience that comes from some deed of ours which is not in accord with God's will or calling in our lives. Guilt itself, however, is NOT bad! In fact, it is actually GOOD, provided that the guilt we are experiencing is "rational" guilt rather than "irrational" guilt.

Rational guilt is the guilt we experience when, yes, we have done something wrong and we know it. The guilt we experience is a good thing because it is intended by God to serve as a self-correcting mechanism. As we sense a lack of peace in our lives, this gnawing feeling (conscience) is a call to look again at ourselves and reflect upon why this is so and what we can do about it.

Staying close to Christ is particularly helpful. For, if instead of looking to Christ, we choose to fill our lives with things (i.e., a new car, job, home, vacation, etc.) to fill this emptiness, we will remain peace-less. In looking to Jesus Christ, however, we again can expect to find "the way, the truth and the life." We can turn around destructive habits and sense an experience of conversion, to which the sacrament of Reconciliation calls us.

Irrational guilt is the feeling we experience in— the following example. You have to make a choice about something very serious, and you just do what you have to do. In coming to your decision, you think about this, you pray, seek the advice, perhaps, of respected others and do some reading to further assist your understanding of the issue. After all of this and finally doing something about this decision, you feel very peaceful and comfortable with what you've done, why you've done it, and the process used in making this decision. Someone, however, comes up to you and declares that your action was immoral or inappropriate or just plain wrong. Then, after listening to that person and reflecting upon what was said and then re-thinking your own process and actions and still sensing that what you did was the good and right action at the time, you start to have feelings that seem very much like guilt. In fact, you are experiencing irrational guilt. This is what we mean when we hear the saying: "laying a guilt trip upon someone."

What do we do? First, we listen caringly to the other person because any Christian should always be attentive whenever he or she is being addressed. Second, we do not let this person's intrusion get to us.

QUESTION: What should I do when my child doesn't even want to talk of God?

RESPONSE: Right now, his/her spirit is closed. We respect them "where they are." We love them to growth. We do this, first of all, by daily prayerfully placing them in the hands of God. With private prayer and our own **good example**, these lost souls may yet be brought to Christ Jesus himself who admonishes us to do the works of God while it is still day (Jn 9:4). We must be patient and kind so that those around us may see the face of Christ and come to know his healing touch.

What did Our Lord say about people who seemed half-pagan? He said they were like sheep without a shepherd, and He had compassion on them (Mk 6:34). We must give such individuals a worthy example.

QUESTION: Where do I turn for help?

RESPONSE: To the Body of Christ: the Eucharist and the Faith Community.

To be disciples of Christ, we must be part of a praying community. The distinguished Anglican, Evelyn Underhill, writes that the founders of the world religions either started a prayer community or already belonged to one. Our Lord belonged to one such praying community, that of the Jews. We sometimes forget that Jesus was a Jew to the core. A community, Underhill writes, keeps disciples on a realistic spiritual road. Our Lord realized that his followers needed a faith community.

Find a prayer group or faith-sharing group in your parish. If your parish doesn't have one, start one!

QUESTION: Any other thoughts on how I might grow in holiness?

RESPONSE: Cardinal Newman once wrote: "If you ask me what you are to do in order to be perfect, I say, first, do not lie in bed beyond the due time of rising; give your first thoughts to God; make an

Angelus; eat and drink to God's glory; say the Rosary well; be recollected; keep out bad thoughts; make your evening meditation well; examine yourself daily; go to bed in good time, and you are already perfect."[12]

Also, at the same time, simply meeting daily responsibilities is important. Teaching class, working in the office, returning calls, cleaning the house, are elements of one's concrete vocation, and one draws close to God by doing them for His greater honor and glory.

QUESTION: Any concluding thoughts?

RESPONSE: Generally speaking, to cope with and grow through any difficult experience in your life:

1. Keep your focus on the Lord, and not on the problem or circumstances.

2. Ask the question, "What is the message you have for me through this experience, Lord?" It's a far more useful question than "Why me?"

3. While keeping your focus on the Lord, begin to look for a positive outcome, which is the Lord's presence, and the Holy Spirit's movement in the experience.

4. Realize that any human being grows in a positive way in and through the experience of love.

5. Be patient ... like St. Monica.

6. When moved by the Holy Spirit, lovingly speak to your loved one of what you get from the Mass and belonging to the Church.

7. When the timing seems right, gently ask

your loved one for reasons for his/her alien-
ation. Initiate a loving dialogue, not a debate.
    8. Service in and for the Church, yourself.
    9. Pray ... a lot

For <u>Lapsed</u> <u>Catholics</u> –

1) Pray for them
2) Be positive in your faith walk!
   Positive **role** model
3) Pray to deepen my trust in God
3 Vacations per day – tell myself –
   I am unique – Valuable – necessary
   + loved by God
Sacramental outlook on <u>ALL</u> of life

Endnotes / Bibliography

[a] These thoughts on forgiveness were contributed with permission of Dr. David Jeremiah in his treatise "The Power of Prayer" from *Turning Point Ministries*, San Diego, California, 1997.

[b] This background information on St. Monica was contributed by Fr. Benedict Groeschel, CFR, "Healing The Original Wound", Servant Publications, Ann Arbor, 1993.

[1] "Confessions of St. Augustine", translated by F.J. Sheed (New York: Sheed and Ward, 1943), Book III, 12,43.

[2] "Confessions", Book IX, 13,163.

[3] "Confessions", Book VIII, 12,179.

[4] "Models of the Church", by Avery Dulles, Doubleday, 1974: Chapter 3.

[5] Peterson, Eugene H. *Five Smooth Stones for Pastoral Work.* Atlanta, John Knox Press, 1980: 114-115

[6] Birch, Bruce C., and Larry L. Rasmussen. *Bible and Ethics in the Christian Life.* Minneapolis, Augusburg Fortress, 1989: 26-27.

[7] Peterson: 154.

[8] St. John Damascene, *De fide orth.* 3,24: 94, 1089c.

[9] Ps 130:1

[10] Rom 8:26

[11] St. Augustine, *Sermo* 56, 6,9: PL 38, 381.

[12] Newman, Cardinal John Henry, *Meditations and Devotions,* (Wheathampstead, Hertfordshire, England: Anthony Clarke Books, 1964): 261.

Sin ⊢⊣⊢⊣⊢⊣⊢⊣⊢⊣⊢⊣⊢⊣ Grace

People + circumstances of every day – How I respond leads me farther in grace or towards sin,

Past △ Future

Maslow says most people do not have mountain top experiences with God because they are NOT in the moment!